A NEW ERA OF U.S.-CHINA RELATIONS?

HEARING

BEFORE THE

SUBCOMMITTEE ON ASIA AND THE PACIFIC

OF THE

COMMITTEE ON FOREIGN AFFAIRS
HOUSE OF REPRESENTATIVES

ONE HUNDRED THIRTEENTH CONGRESS

SECOND SESSION

SEPTEMBER 17, 2014

Serial No. 113–216

Printed for the use of the Committee on Foreign Affairs

Available via the World Wide Web: http://www.foreignaffairs.house.gov/ or
http://www.gpo.gov/fdsys/

U.S. GOVERNMENT PRINTING OFFICE

89–813PDF   WASHINGTON : 2014

For sale by the Superintendent of Documents, U.S. Government Printing Office
Internet: bookstore.gpo.gov   Phone: toll free (866) 512–1800; DC area (202) 512–1800
Fax: (202) 512–2104   Mail: Stop IDCC, Washington, DC 20402–0001

COMMITTEE ON FOREIGN AFFAIRS

EDWARD R. ROYCE, California, *Chairman*

CHRISTOPHER H. SMITH, New Jersey
ILEANA ROS-LEHTINEN, Florida
DANA ROHRABACHER, California
STEVE CHABOT, Ohio
JOE WILSON, South Carolina
MICHAEL T. McCAUL, Texas
TED POE, Texas
MATT SALMON, Arizona
TOM MARINO, Pennsylvania
JEFF DUNCAN, South Carolina
ADAM KINZINGER, Illinois
MO BROOKS, Alabama
TOM COTTON, Arkansas
PAUL COOK, California
GEORGE HOLDING, North Carolina
RANDY K. WEBER SR., Texas
SCOTT PERRY, Pennsylvania
STEVE STOCKMAN, Texas
RON DeSANTIS, Florida
DOUG COLLINS, Georgia
MARK MEADOWS, North Carolina
TED S. YOHO, Florida
SEAN DUFFY, Wisconsin
CURT CLAWSON, Florida

ELIOT L. ENGEL, New York
ENI F.H. FALEOMAVAEGA, American
 Samoa
BRAD SHERMAN, California
GREGORY W. MEEKS, New York
ALBIO SIRES, New Jersey
GERALD E. CONNOLLY, Virginia
THEODORE E. DEUTCH, Florida
BRIAN HIGGINS, New York
KAREN BASS, California
WILLIAM KEATING, Massachusetts
DAVID CICILLINE, Rhode Island
ALAN GRAYSON, Florida
JUAN VARGAS, California
BRADLEY S. SCHNEIDER, Illinois
JOSEPH P. KENNEDY III, Massachusetts
AMI BERA, California
ALAN S. LOWENTHAL, California
GRACE MENG, New York
LOIS FRANKEL, Florida
TULSI GABBARD, Hawaii
JOAQUIN CASTRO, Texas

AMY PORTER, *Chief of Staff*   THOMAS SHEEHY, *Staff Director*
JASON STEINBAUM, *Democratic Staff Director*

———

SUBCOMMITTEE ON ASIA AND THE PACIFIC

STEVE CHABOT, Ohio, *Chairman*

DANA ROHRABACHER, California
MATT SALMON, Arizona
MO BROOKS, Alabama
GEORGE HOLDING, North Carolina
SCOTT PERRY, Pennsylvania
DOUG COLLINS, Georgia
CURT CLAWSON, Florida

ENI F.H. FALEOMAVAEGA, American
 Samoa
AMI BERA, California
TULSI GABBARD, Hawaii
BRAD SHERMAN, California
GERALD E. CONNOLLY, Virginia
WILLIAM KEATING, Massachusetts

CONTENTS

A NEW ERA OF U.S.–CHINA RELATIONS?

WEDNESDAY, SEPTEMBER 17, 2014

House of Representatives,
Subcommittee on Asia and the Pacific,
Committee on Foreign Affairs,
Washington, DC.

The committee met, pursuant to notice, at 2:30 p.m., in room 2172 Rayburn House Office Building, Hon. Steve Chabot (chairman of the subcommittee) presiding.

Mr. CHABOT. Good afternoon, and welcome to this afternoon's subcommittee hearing. I want to thank our distinguished witnesses for being here as we examine a critical relationship that is becoming increasingly challenging and unfortunately confrontational—and one that surely deserves more attention.

The nature of the United States' relationship with the People's Republic of China has arguably entered a new era. Since President Xi Jinping assumed the leadership role in China, U.S.-China affairs have steadily undergone a fundamental transformation. In this new era, the PRC is more assertive and, indeed, aggressive on an entire range of issues covering the political, security, and socioeconomic spectrums.

Today, we hope to learn more about China's new leadership team and discuss what we can do as a nation to ensure that America's interests are best represented overseas.

I believe that the U.S.-China relationship is one of our most important given what is at stake. And when we discuss what exactly is at stake—such as peace and security across the Taiwan Strait and freedom of navigation and movement in the East China and South China Seas—we see that not enough attention is being given to this critical relationship.

Just a few months ago, the debate focused on whether the administration's "pivot to Asia" was adequately resourced. Today, I believe that this "pivot" is stuttering. When it comes to the Asia-Pacific region, the conversation is focused on China, and this includes China's aggressive foray into the South China Seas. It's clear the administration is struggling to find a way to better direct America's resources toward the Asia-Pacific and find a way to manage the growth of maritime territorial disputes. As a result, with this void, we see that China is shifting its assertiveness in the security arena and is now focusing it on American businesses operating in that country.

According to a recent article in the New York Times, "foreign companies in a range of industries including automobiles, technology, pharmaceuticals and food packaging have faced increased scrutiny including raids and allegations of unfair practices.'' The article goes on to say that the heightened attention against foreign companies—including many American firms—comes at a time when Beijing is looking for ways to help its homegrown industries. I find this behavior particularly troubling given that it violates China's own commitments to the World Trade Organization.

China's increased level of enforcement activity comes from the implementation of its Antimonopoly Law, which was drafted over a period of 10 years in consultation with authorities in the U.S. Government and the European Union. The law even draws from elements of both U.S. and EU competition laws. But, now, it's being used to target U.S. and EU companies. During the U.S.-China Security and Economic Dialogue held this past July, China committed to using its monopoly laws to promote consumer welfare and not its domestic companies or industries. This is not what we are seeing happen.

China's National Development and Reform Commission, the organization responsible for reviewing monopoly activities, abuse of dominance, and abuse of administrative power involving pricing, asserts that foreign companies only account for 10 percent of antimonopoly cases. However, this can't be verified and the situation seems anything but fair, objective, transparent, or nondiscriminatory.

Earlier this month, the U.S.-China Business Council reported that 86 percent of its member companies are concerned about China's evolving antimonopoly regime. Among the many reasons are broader concerns about how China will use this law to protect domestic industry, how it will affect the value of intellectual property, and whether it will be used to force lower prices rather than let the market decide. As a result, in addition to already growing concerns about China cyberhacking offensive, warming relations with Russia, and aggressive incursion upon the territories claimed by neighboring nations, the implications of China's antimonopoly investigations could be quite serious.

In my congressional district in southwestern, Ohio which includes the city of Cincinnati, a significant number of businesses count on the Chinese market for an important part of their annual sales. Small businesses and large businesses alike, exports to China have helped many firms grow and prosper—and hire American workers. However, as reports about China's antimonopoly investigations mount, so do worries about the unfair treatment of U.S. businesses in that country.

Looking ahead, it's vital that we gain a better understanding of the Chinese leadership, and its political, security, and socio-economic goals. It's also critical for us to determine a way forward for effectively engaging with various stakeholders in China so that the U.S. businesses have a clearer understanding about what this means for their future activities in China. What is at stake in this new era of U.S.-China relations is extremely important and now is the time to give it the attention it deserves. I look forward to the testimonies of the witnesses here this afternoon, and I would now like to recognize the ranking member of this subcommittee, Eni Faleomavaega from American Samoa.

Mr. FALEOMAVAEGA. Thank you, Mr. Chairman. And I want to thank you for holding today's hearing on U.S.-China relations. This is an important opportunity for our subcommittee to review and evaluate our relationship with China as we move forward in the coming years.

I especially want to thank my good friend and dear colleague, the congressman from California, for all these years that we have been butting heads too, and deeply enjoyed his input and understanding of the issues affecting the Asia-Pacific region. And I also personally welcome Mr. Johnson and Mr. Chang as our witnesses this morning.

As China's economy continues to rise and the U.S. economy stagnates, there is no doubt that China will overtake the U.S. as the world's largest economy soon. China remains the largest manufacturer, the largest trading economy, and also holds the largest foreign exchange reserves in the world.

China's economic growth is also driving the demand for energy for a population of almost 1.4 billion people. This is a direct impact on world energy markets. China will likely be the world's largest importer of oil, and is heavily relying on other countries to provide long term energy resources, like natural gas and oil pipelines from Russia and Central Asia as well as the influx of Chinese investments for steady oil supply from Africa.

A greater concern for economic and strategic security is the significant increase in spending by China to beef up its military and develop more high tech weapons. With the expansion of China's naval and improvements in its defense and missile capabilities, this buildup may be a direct threat to countries like Japan, Vietnam, the Philippines, and others which are engaged in territorial disputes with China in the South China Sea and East China Seas. Although military ties between the U.S. and China have strengthened and engagement has increased in the past few years, the United States is pivoting to Asia as a counter.

Are we too late, Mr. Chairman? For years I have been critical of U.S. foreign policy toward the Asia-Pacific region, because for too long the United States has neglected a part of the world where two thirds of the world's population resides and which includes, according to the United States Pacific Command, seven of the world's ten largest standing militaries, five of the world's declared nuclear nations, two of three largest economies, and the largest democracy, the world's busiest international sea lanes and nine of the ten largest ports, all in the Asia-Pacific region.

So while I appreciate the need for the United States to focus on Europe and the Middle East, given the complexities in those regions I am disappointed that the United States has failed to devote the same time, attention and resources to the Asia-Pacific region where we are also faced with unique and complex challenges that also seriously affect U.S. security and stability.

For your information, Mr. Chairman, many of American Samoa's sons and daughters as well as military men and women from your district proudly serve in the U.S. Pacific Command to protect and defend the territory of the United States, its people and its interest in the Asia-Pacific region and they deserve more than a pivot as do Pacific Island nations.

Pacific Island nations supported U.S. interest during World War II, but when times got good for us we neglect them also. Now China is providing hundreds of millions of dollars in aid to help their struggling economies and improve their quality of life.

Many Pacific Island nations including American Samoa's closest neighbor, the Independent State of Samoa, is accepting China's assistance. Many Island nations' leaders have no choice but to work and strengthen their partnerships with China, and I don't blame them given that the United States has been an undependable partner.

It is very unfortunate, Mr. Chairman, that the United States, Australia and New Zealand are just now realizing how important the Asia-Pacific region is. But as the Pentagon finally shifts its posture for rebalancing in the Asia-Pacific region, it is my sincere hope that the administration will not only take a look at engaging China and improving bilateral relations that would be beneficial to both countries, but I also hope that we will seriously go about in strengthening our relationships with our allies and partners throughout the Asia-Pacific region. I also hope we will address the concerns of our U.S. business community overseas.

With that, Mr. Chairman, again I thank you for your leadership and for taking this time to hold this hearing, and again I welcome our witnesses this morning. Thank you.

Mr. CHABOT. Thank you very much. The gentleman yields back. And I would now like to recognize the gentleman from California, Mr. Rohrabacher, who also is the chairman of the Subcommittee on Europe, Eurasia, and Emerging Threats, for the purpose of making an opening statement.

Mr. ROHRABACHER. Thank you very much, and I will treat this as not a new era but an emerging threat.

I want to thank the chairman and thank my good friend, Eni Faleomavaega. And it took me a long, long time to learn how to pronounce that name, but it was worth it because Eni has been one of the great, great members of this body and who has won the hearts and respect of people on both sides of the aisle. So we are very happy to celebrate your leadership as well, Eni.

Today we are of course looking at China. And let me just give this challenge to the leadership in China who I hope are listening. They usually do pay attention to hearings like this. If you want us to believe that you are reforming, do something that you can do that will indicate that you are taking a major step in the right direction.

And that would be, I would suggest, that you declare that it is no longer the policy of the Communist Party of China to discourage the worship of God and that you now respect the freedom of people to worship God in their own way.

That is a very doable thing for them. It would not in any way put them in harm's way. If they can't do that they can't reform anyway politically and socially in that country. We have Falun Gong who are still being arrested in great numbers and murdered in prison, their organs sold; Muslims who are being repressed; Buddhist monasteries in Tibet that are still suffering, and Buddhist priests that are treated so badly they are committing suicide, burning themselves to death. And then of course we have the control of Christian churches so that they have strict controls of what is going on.

This is something they can do. If they want to—look, we know there are no opposition parties. There is no freedom of press. There is no freedom of demonstrations. There is no labor unions. There is no independent court system in China for this new day. But if they want to show us that they are going in the right direction, they can't cure all of that or maybe even one of those might be too much, but at least walk away from this idea that you have got to repress people when they are worshiping God. And that is the challenge of today.

I am interested in hearing the witnesses, and especially in terms of the military actions that China has taken, the rogue China that now threatens the territorial claims against Japan, the Philippines, Vietnam and India. Thank you very much, Mr. Chairman.

Mr. CHABOT. Thank you very much, Mr. Chairman. And I have been advised that we have visitors with us today from the American Chamber of Commerce in Shanghai, and the subcommittee would like to welcome you; we hope that your visit is productive. And if you would like to stand and be recognized we would encourage you to do so. [Applause.]

Thank you for spending some time with us. And I would now like to introduce our distinguished panel here this afternoon before we hear their testimony.

First, Mr. Christopher Johnson is a senior adviser and holds the Freeman chair in China Studies at the Center for Strategic and International Studies. Previously, Mr. Johnson worked as a senior China analyst at the CIA. Mr. Johnson served as an intelligence liaison to two Secretaries of State on worldwide security issues, and in 2011 was awarded the U.S. Department of State's Superior Honor Award for outstanding support to the Secretary. He has also served abroad in Southeast Asia. Throughout his career, Mr. Johnson has focused on China's political and economic transformation, the development of its military, and its resurgence as a regional and global power. He has frequently advised senior U.S. policymakers and foreign officials on Chinese leadership and Beijing's foreign and security policies. Mr. Johnson graduated summa cum laude with bachelor's degrees in history and political science from the University of California at San Diego and received his M.A. in security policy studies from the George Washington University. We welcome you this afternoon, Mr. Johnson.

I would next like to introduce Gordon Chang. Mr. Chang is the author of the ''Coming Collapse of China'' and ''Nuclear Showdown: North Korea Takes On the World,'' which focuses on nuclear proliferation and the North Korean crisis. He is a regular contributor at Forbes.com and blogs to the World Affairs Journal. Mr. Chang has worked in China and Hong Kong and most recently in Shanghai as counsel to the American law firm Paul Weiss, and earlier in Hong Kong as partner in the international law firm Baker and McKenzie. His writings have appeared in numerous publications and he is a frequent speaker at universities, think tanks, and private institutions. Mr. Chang has briefed several government agencies and has testified before the House Committee on Foreign Affairs and the U.S.-China Economic and Security Review Commission. He has also served two terms as a trustee of Cornell University. We welcome you here this afternoon, Mr. Chang.

I am sure both witnesses are familiar with the 5-minute rule. We would ask that you keep your testimony within that time. There should be a yellow light that comes on and lets you know when you have 1 minute to wrap up; and the red light will come on. Then we would appreciate it if you would conclude your testimony as close to that time as possible.

And we will begin with you, Mr. Johnson. You are recognized for 5 minutes.

STATEMENT OF MR. CHRISTOPHER K. JOHNSON, SENIOR ADVISER AND FREEMAN CHAIR IN CHINA STUDIES, CENTER FOR STRATEGIC AND INTERNATIONAL STUDIES

Mr. JOHNSON. Thank you very much, Mr. Chairman.

Distinguished members of the subcommittee, good afternoon, and thank you for this opportunity to come before you today. I am especially pleased to know that as was mentioned in some of your opening statements that despite the complex challenges the United States currently is facing in other parts of the world, there is an eagerness among the members to discuss these important issues with regard to the future trajectory of U.S.-China ties under the leadership of its new President, President Xi Jinping.

Although these other challenges that we are facing represent issues of concern and even a clear and present danger to U.S. interests and the lives of our citizens, I would submit that they ultimately should be viewed as near term tactical issues to be skillfully managed by U.S. policymakers. By contrast, getting our relationship with China right should represent the fundamental strategic preoccupation of U.S. foreign policy thinkers in the 21st century.

So let me spend just a few minutes sketching out for you my assessment of the state-of-play in the relationship as well as some of the specific issues that I have been asked by the subcommittee to address in this testimony.

In terms of the relationship, the bilateral relationship, relations between Washington and Beijing while generally stable are certainly under stress. Chinese leaders and officials are at best confused by what they see as a lack of consistency from the Obama administration with regard to its policy toward China, and at worst convinced that the United States is bent on containing China's rise.

For their part, U.S. policymakers are deeply concerned by Beijing's exceptionally forthright assertion of its sovereignty claims to disputed territories in the East and South China Seas, as well as the new Chinese leadership's seemingly more active foreign policy approach in regions outside China's traditional areas of foreign policy interest and focus as China reasserts itself as a global power.

Add to these persistent U.S. concerns with regard to Chinese cyberespionage and the litany of thorny economic issues between our two countries and it is easy to see why the relationship appears more tense than it has in some time. Moreover, senior officials in both capitals bemoan the lack of meaningful strategic dialogue between the two leaderships.

The practical implications of this absence of effective senior level dialogue is the absence of strategic trust between the two leaderships and the resultant drift in bilateral ties brought on by policy stagnation. Still, in my assessment none of these trends is irreversible. It simply requires leadership and a commitment on both sides to building a truly new style of relations between the two nations going forward.

Finally, the traditional conceptions and cadence of the relationship still are adjusting to the phenomenon that is the leadership of Xi Jinping. While certainly no strong man within the Chinese system, Xi is without question the most powerful Chinese leader to emerge in several decades.

Although it is far too early in his tenure to be able to predict with any certainty the precise ramifications of his particular brand of foreign policy making, one thing is perfectly clear. Xi is not responding to the traditional messaging and cueing that being employed by the United States on issues such as tensions in the East and South China Seas, or at least he is not doing so in a way that the U.S. Government would like him to.

This reality does not necessarily demand a specific set of policy responses from the United States, but it should give U.S. policymakers pause and a desire to reflect on whether, and how, U.S. actions may need to be recalibrated to deal with this fundamentally different approach from the Chinese leader.

Turning to the prospects for economic reform inside China, it is fair to say that the reform progress has struggled in the first half of this year. And this can be ascribed to several factors including a recognition on the part of Xi Jinping and his economic team that the scale of the challenge is much greater and the resistance that they face is far more entrenched than they might earlier have assessed.

Another factor is the pervasive fear that has been engendered among working level officialdom as a result of Xi Jinping's anticorruption drive. Officials have been in a near state of paralysis for fear that they may somehow be swept up in the campaign. Against this backdrop, few in the working level bureaucracy have been inclined to offer up radical reform proposals.

Finally, the economy's sluggish performance also has acted as a drag on reform progress. This will provide all the more incentive for the government to adopt additional stimulus measures for the final quarter of the year in order to meet the leadership's ambitious annual growth target of 7.5 percent.

Such pressures and practices risk crowding out the room for reform headway as officials, especially at the local level, single-mindedly batten down the hatches to be able to weather the storm that they are facing.

Still, there are reasons to believe that prospects for reform progress at the end of this year and going into 2015 may be brightening. For example, it will be important for the leadership to set the right tone on the pace of reform before the Communist Party's economic planners begin focusing in earnest on drafting the 13th Five-Year Plan which will be approved at a fall plenum next year.

And finally, let me turn to this issue of market conditions facing foreign companies operating in China. The environment confronting foreign companies doing business in China has changed substantially in the wake of the 2008 global financial crisis. In this year's business confidence study conducted by AmCham China, for example, 40 percent of respondents perceive that foreign companies are being singled out in the pricing and antitrust investigations that now are touching a very wide array of industries operating inside the country.

There is no one clear answer concerning what may be driving these pressure tactics, though the pattern that emerges from a close look at the investigations being conducted suggests that they are motivated by some combination of an understandable desire to bring prices down, traditional rent-seeking behavior and some element of bureaucratic competition between the Chinese Government entities charged with overseeing the investigations.

Still, these explanations though certainly part of the puzzle are dwarfed by a single, overarching priority of the regime, the preservation and strengthening of China's unique state capitalist system. In fact, the regulatory agencies appear to be designing a template with these investigations with potential applicability across a wide variety of industries.

The specific measures taken will vary on a case-by-case basis, but it is likely to involve a combination of several techniques including the threat of price investigations to win concessions, the use of investigations often in tandem with well coordinated exposes by state-controlled media to mar the reputational standing of the targeted firm, and the provision of subsidies and the promotion of consolidation of domestic producers in the targeted industry to boost the competitiveness of designated so-called national champions.

Going forward, we can expect that China will continue to use all the tools at its disposal including selective enforcement of rules, provision of subsidies, and technology transfer requirements to create an environment that unduly favors the development of its domestic champions.

And with that I will cease there and yield back to the chair. Thank you.

[The prepared statement of Mr. Johnson follows:]

CSIS | CENTER FOR STRATEGIC &
INTERNATIONAL STUDIES

Statement before the House Committee on
Foreign Affairs, Subcommittee on Asia and the Pacific

"A NEW ERA OF U.S.-CHINA RELATIONS?"

A Statement by:

Christopher K. Johnson

Senior Adviser and Freeman Chair in China Studies

Center for Strategic and International Studies (CSIS)

September 17, 2014

2127 Rayburn House Office Building

WWW.CSIS.ORG   1616 RHODE ISLAND AVENUE NW,   TEL (202) 887.0200
WASHINGTON, DC 20036   FAX (202) 775.3199

Distinguished members of the Subcommittee,

Good afternoon, and thank you for this opportunity to come before you today. I'm especially pleased to know that, despite the complex challenges the United States currently is facing with ISIS in Iraq and Syria, as well as Russia's brinksmanship with the West over Ukraine, there is an eagerness among the members to discuss these important issues with regard to the future trajectory of U.S.-China ties under the leadership of Chinese President Xi Jinping. Although these other challenges represent issues of concern, and, in the case of ISIS, a clear and present danger to U.S. interests and the lives of our citizens, I would submit that they ultimately should be viewed as near-term, **tactical** issues to be skillfully managed by policymakers. By contrast, getting our relationship with China right should represent the fundamental **strategic** preoccupation of U.S. foreign policy thinkers in the 21st Century. So let me spend a few moments sketching out for you my assessment of the state-of-play in the relationship as well as some of the specific issues I've been asked by the Subcommittee to address in this testimony.

Overview of the State of U.S.-China Relations

Relations between Washington and Beijing, while generally stable, are under stress. Chinese leaders and officials are at best confused by what they see as a lack of consistency from the Obama Administration with regard to its policy toward China, and at worst convinced that the United States, in large part through the rebalance—or "pivot"—to Asia, is bent on containing China's rise through destabilizing the Chinese Communist Party (CCP) leadership at home and seeking, in conjunction with its allies and partners, to place hard limits on China's strategic freedom of action in the Asia-Pacific region. For their part, U.S. policymakers are deeply concerned by Beijing's exceptionally forthright assertion of its sovereignty claims to disputed territories in the East and South China Seas, as well as the new Chinese leadership's seemingly more active—some would say disruptive—foreign policy approach in regions outside China's traditional areas of foreign policy interest and focus. Add to these persistent U.S. concerns with regard to Chinese cyberespionage and, in the bilateral economic relationship, issues relating to intellectual property rights (IPR) protection, currency valuation, and market access, and it is easy to see why the relationship appears more tense than it has in some time.

Moreover, senior officials in both capitals bemoan the lack of meaningful strategic dialogue between the two leaderships. This is despite the informal summit between the two presidents at the Sunnylands retreat in California a little over a year ago—set to be repeated on the Chinese side when President Obama visits for the APEC summit in November—and the existence of more formal, high-level dialogue channels between the two sides such as the Strategic and Economic Dialogue (S&ED). Some of this relates to personalities. There is a general consensus that there is very little observable chemistry between Presidents Obama and Xi, especially when compared to Xi's seemingly solid relationship with Russian President Vladimir Putin.

At the next level down, the Chinese generally view their S&ED interlocutors as largely disinterested in Asia or too domestically-focused. Similarly, on the U.S. side, there are questions about portfolio mismatch arising from the fact that, unlike his predecessor, Wang Qishan, Vice Premier Wang Yang, Treasury Secretary Lew's counterpart, does not oversee financial affairs within the Chinese State Council, or cabinet. Likewise, there are uncertainties about whether Secretary of State Kerry's interlocutor, State Councilor Yang Jiechi, commands the same level of authority over foreign affairs management that his predecessor, Dai Bingguo, seemed to wield.

The practical implications of a set of such relationships that frequently seem out of sync is the absence of strategic trust between the two leaderships and the resultant drift in bilateral ties brought on by policy stagnation. This year's S&ED would seem a case in point. If that mechanism were functioning normally, it would have been used as a crucial policy springboard for paving the way for an important summit between the two presidents, especially one where Xi, as a still relatively untested ruler, is keen to show off his foreign policy acumen in playing host to all of the region's most important leaders at the APEC summit. Instead, the meeting released a relatively bland series of pronouncements which, after the summer in both capitals and an intense focus early in the fall on critical domestic events in each country, leaves precious little time to think about policy solutions for elevating the relationship at the summit. Still, none of these trends is irreversible; it simply requires leadership and a commitment on both sides to building a **truly** new style or relations between the two nations going forward.

Finally, the traditional conceptions and cadence of the relationship still are adjusting to the phenomenon that is the leadership of Xi Jinping. While certainly no strongman, Xi is without question the most powerful Chinese leader to emerge in several decades. Two primary factors should command our attention in understanding that Xi's personal preoccupations, and, perhaps occasionally, even his musings are likely to play an outsize role in governing China's foreign policy approach, including relations with Washington, during his tenure. First, Xi has skillfully wielded an often coercive political toolkit to accrete tremendous power to himself in a very short period of time. Second, his perception of himself as a "doer" or a "man of action" means that his appetite for risk, both domestically and externally, is substantially higher than that of his immediate predecessors. His innate confidence as a leader and reliance on an informal, "kitchen cabinet" style of policy advisory means that decision making under him is likely to be more opaque—and far less deliberative—than before.

Although it is far too early in his tenure to be able to predict with any certainty the precise ramifications of his particular brand of foreign policy making, one thing is perfectly clear. Xi is not responding to the traditional messaging and cueing being employed by the United States on issues such as tensions in the East and South China Seas, or at least he is not doing so in the way the U.S. Government would like him to. This reality does not necessarily demand a specific set of policy responses from the United States, but it should give U.S. policymakers pause and a desire to reflect on whether—and how—U.S. actions may need to be recalibrated to deal with this fundamentally different approach. It also suggests that traditional assessments concerning indicators and warning of potentially disruptive Chinese actions may need to be revisited in a much more fluid Chinese policy environment where the previous utility of such tools may be substantially diminished.

Assessment of the Status of and Prospects for Economic Reform

Following on the sense of optimism—and even euphoria—coming out of the bold economic reform vision statement that was tabled by the leadership and endorsed by the Central Committee at last fall's Third Plenum, it is fair to say that reform progress has struggled in the first half of this year. This can be ascribed to several interrelated factors. One is what appears to be a recalibration of the approach by Xi and his team of economic advisors resulting from the collision between unrealistic expectations and political realities. Xi and his supporters seem initially to have believed that they could simply overwhelm the regime's many vested interests through a form of economic "shock and awe" that combined bold reform prescriptions with the Plenum's establishment of a new supra-leading group on deepening reform to guide—and enforce—the process. They have since recognized that the scale of the challenge is much greater and the resistance is far more entrenched. Having concluded that he will need more than "the big idea" and some bureaucratic hijinks to achieve his aims, there are several signs that Xi is at least considering a more transformational approach to undermine his detractors. This would entail putting on hold many of the readily observable reform proposals, such as a deposit insurance scheme or the liberalization of deposit rates, to focus instead on promoting governance reforms that could amount to a reshaping of the party-state to promote his administration's stated goal of assigning the market a "decisive role" in the economy.

Another factor is the pervasive fear that has been engendered among working-level officialdom as a result of the aggressiveness of Xi's anticorruption drive. Officials have been in a near state of paralysis for fear that they may somehow be swept up in the campaign through a particular decision or expression of support for a reform project or action. The bureaucracy also would be aware that Xi had been stoking substantial resentment on the part of other powerful party barons—most notably former President Jiang Zemin—by targeting their support networks with the antigraft campaign. Against this backdrop, few in the working-level bureaucracy have been inclined to offer up radical reform proposals when it was so abundantly clear that there was discord among the senior leadership, and that the outcome of that struggle was not clear cut.

Finally, the economy's sluggish performance also has acted as a drag on reform progress. The deeply disappointing industrial production figures just released for August—where growth slowed to its lowest level since the 2008 global financial crisis—are but one indication of the malaise that seems to have grabbed hold of certain parts of the economy. This will provide all the more incentive for the government to adopt additional stimulus measures for the final quarter of the year in order to meet the leadership's annual growth target of 7.5 percent set in March. Such pressures and practices risk crowding out the room for reform headway as officials, especially at the local level, single-mindedly batten down the hatches to be able to weather the storm.

Still, there are reasons to believe that prospects for reform progress at the end of this year and going into 2015 may be brightening. With the netting of two major "tigers" (Xi's political catchphrase for senior corrupt officials) in recent months as part of the antigraft crusade, there is some sense that at least the worst of the high-level political tensions in the system may be unwinding enough that officials feel they can start taking some more risks. Similarly, it will be important for the leadership to set the right tone on the pace of reform before the Communist Party's economic planners begin focusing in earnest on drafting the 13th Five-Year Plan which will be approved at next year's plenum. Given that the Plan's life span (2016-2020) will expire precisely when the leadership has set out a major strategic benchmark for achieving "meaningful progress" on the reforms, we can expect Xi, whose legacy will in part be judged by what has been accomplished, will be keen to keep officials' feet to the fire. Moreover, just by the natural cycling of the Chinese political calendar, Xi and his cohort have at most another eighteen months to make substantial progress before the political horse trading begins again in earnest ahead of the next party congress in 2017.

Review of the Market Conditions Facing Foreign Companies Operating in China

The environment confronting foreign companies doing business in China has changed substantially in the wake of the 2008 global financial crisis. The altered landscape is perhaps best reflected in shifting response patterns to annual surveys of the sentiments of business leaders working in China and conducted by their host nation chambers of commerce. While recent surveys have continued to highlight traditional areas of concern such as rising labor costs and inconsistent or unclear laws and regulations, respondents to this year's surveys zeroed in on challenges that they claimed impact foreign business disproportionately. According to the study conducted by AmCham China, for example, fewer respondents than ever believe that licenses are granted equally between foreign and Chinese companies, a strong majority of respondents still characterize IPR enforcement in China as ineffective, and 40 percent of respondents perceive that foreign companies are being singled out in the pricing and antitrust investigations that now are touching a very wide array of industries operating in the country.

There is no one clear answer concerning what may be driving these pressure tactics, and the motives do seem to vary somewhat by industry. In the case of pricing investigations, it is not surprising that products like pharmaceuticals and infant milk powder have been targeted. The central leadership understands full well that it is staring down the barrel of a trillion dollar health care bill by 2020 as it dramatically expands coverage for China's massive population, and there is no doubt that the message has gone down from the leadership to the entire state bureaucracy to do whatever it takes to bring down costs.

In other instances, the motivation appears to be as simple as traditional rent-seeking behavior, or the perception that a substantial financial windfall lies within easy reach. Looking just at the investigation into GlaxoSmithKline, for example, it is hard to imagine that Chinese authorities weren't inspired, at least in part, by the company's agreeing to pay $3 billion in fines to settle fraud charges in the United States. Lastly, we also cannot discount the impact of simple bureaucratic rivalry in explaining the uptick in reports from foreign firms alleging various strong-arm tactics by Chinese regulators. The fact that there are three separate Chinese government entities—the National Development and Reform Commission (NDRC), the Ministry of Commerce (MOFCOM) and the State Administration of Industry and Commerce (SAIC)—competing for dominance in what clearly is a senior leadership-favored policy domain helps at some level to explain the seeming emergence of bureaucratic one-upsmanship between these bodies in their approach to these various types of investigations. In fact, proposals being debated in Chinese policy circles concerning a possible consolidation of these responsibilities under a single authority would suggest that the competition among these regulatory bodies—and concomitantly the pressure on foreign firms—may only intensify going forward.

Still, these explanations, though certainly part of the puzzle, are dwarfed by a single overarching priority of the regime—the preservation and strengthening of China's unique state capitalist system. To some degree, the probes can therefore be understood as the central leadership's effort to reassure the state behemoths as, in keeping with the Third Plenum's pronouncements, the Communist Party deliberates greater liberalization in several previously protected industries. Moreover, and in conjunction with the dramatic expansion of their administrative toolkit, the regulatory agencies appear to be designing a template with these investigations with potential applicability across a wide variety of industries. The specific measures taken will vary on a case by case basis, but it is likely to involve a combination of several techniques, including the threat of price investigations to win concessions; the use of investigations or well-coordinated "exposes" by state controlled media to mar the reputational standing of the targeted firm; and the provision of subsidies and the promotion of consolidation of domestic producers in the targeted industry to boost the competitiveness of designated national champions. Going forward, we can expect that China will continue to use all of the tools at its disposal—including selective enforcement of rules, provision of subsidies, and technology transfer requirements—to create an environment that unduly favors the development of its domestic champions.

———————

Mr. CHABOT. Thank you very much.

Mr. Chang, you are recognized for 5 minutes.

STATEMENT OF MR. GORDON CHANG, AUTHOR

Mr. CHANG. Chairman Chabot, Ranking Member Faleoma-vaega—and I hope I pronounced that correctly and I apologize if I didn't——

Mr. FALEOMAVAEGA. You said it just right, John Wayne.

Mr. CHANG [continuing]. And distinguished members of the committee, it is a privilege for me to appear before you today.

Mr. CHABOT. Just for the record, you mispronounced my name, but that is okay.

Mr. CHANG. I apologize.

Mr. CHABOT. It is Chabot, like in S–H, even though it is C–H, but everybody mispronounces it, so there you go. So nobody can win around here, Eni.

Mr. CHANG. It is a privilege for me to appear before you today and I thank you for this opportunity. My testimony focuses on the highly discriminatory antimonopoly enforcement against foreign companies in China, and there are three reasons why we need to be concerned.

First, China's obviously unfair application of its laws in this area is illustrative of common themes of foreign business in China. Second, this campaign complicates already deteriorating China-U.S. relations. And finally, the fundamental reason that Beijing engages in this campaign suggests that relations between China and the U.S. over the long term will remain troubled. And I will direct my testimony to the last point.

There has always been some hostility in China toward foreign business, but new ruler Xi Jinping has taken it to a new level. So, for instance, in July of last year, the National Development and Reform Commission, which is one of three of China's competition regulators, forced these companies, about 30 of them, into a room for 2 days and wanted them to write self-criticisms.

Since then, the campaign against American companies has been unrelenting. Microsoft is the current target, but QualComm could be wounded, perhaps seriously, because China is targeting its most important source of revenue. And Time Magazine, in July, asked, is no foreign brand safe in China? And unfortunately the answer is, no brand is safe. And the question we need to ask is why?

Well, many say that this is just a squabble over market share with increasingly powerful state enterprises wanting to take business away from foreign companies. Now of course there is more to it than that. The campaign against foreign business almost certainly is directed from the top of the Chinese political system, the seven-member Politburo Standing Committee of the Communist Party, because nothing this important in China could go on for so long unless it had approval from the top of the system.

The campaign unfortunately is a frontal attack on foreign business and it brings to mind the xenophobia of the Maoist area because Xi Jinping has been conducting a series of Maoist inspired rectification and mass line campaigns since he took over as China's leader in November 2012. Now the use of Cultural Revolution style methods against multinationals suggests that this Maoist rhetoric is actually starting to affect Chinese governance.

Now Chinese leaders are not acting pragmatically right now, that is because of the nature of the Chinese political system. And despite all the reform and progress that we have seen today, China is still driven by the need to seek to, first and foremost, legitimize the Communist Party. Xi Jinping, I believe, is trying to legitimize the Party not only by attacking foreigners, but also he is attacking foreigners to help him consolidate what I believe is a shaky political position at home.

So political considerations are driving the Chinese leaders to go after us, and in all likelihood I believe that this campaign will intensify at least in the long term. The fault is in the nature of the Chinese political system which no Chinese leader is prepared to change. And in this highly charged political environment, it is not likely that China can maintain good relations with its neighbors, with the international community, with the United States. It is clear that considering everything that Xi Jinping will not stop this campaign until the U.S. Government impose costs on China that are greater than the benefits that China gets from discriminating against U.S. companies.

With China's growing reliance on exports, Washington has the leverage to stop China in its tracks. For instance, last year, China's overall merchandise trade surplus against the United States which was a record $318.7 billion was a stunning 122.7 percent of China's overall surplus. We can find other locations to manufacture goods, and in fact that process is happening already. But China cannot replace the U.S. market.

We can protect our companies by limiting China's access to our market through special tariffs and other mechanisms but it is clear that we have to do something. Our companies and our workers are already bleeding. Thank you.

[The prepared statement of Mr. Chang follows:]

**Statement of
Gordon G. Chang**

**Subcommittee on
Asia and the Pacific
House Committee on Foreign Affairs**

A New Era of U.S.-China Relations?

September 17, 2014

Chairman Chabot, Ranking Member Faleomavaega, and distinguished Members of the Committee:

It is a privilege for me to appear before you today, and I thank you for this opportunity.

My name is Gordon Guthrie Chang. I am a writer and live in Bedminster, New Jersey. I worked as a lawyer in Hong Kong from 1981-1991 and Shanghai from 1996-2001. Between these two periods, I frequently traveled to Asia from California. I regularly go there now.

I am the author of *The Coming Collapse of China* (Random House, 2001) and *Nuclear Showdown: North Korea Takes On the World* (Random House, 2006). I write regularly about China's economy and politics for Forbes and other publications.

China's Long-Term Campaign Against Foreign Companies

During what is known as the "reform era"—the period beginning at the end of 1978 until now—the People's Republic of China sought the technology, expertise, and know-how of foreign companies. Reformist leaders realized that, to obtain what they wanted, they would have to allow these companies to have access to the Chinese market.

Now, however, Chinese leaders, often pressed by politically powerful state enterprises, believe they have enough leverage to take back their market from foreign competitors. Severe turmoil in Beijing political circles aggravates the plight of foreigners as do the regressive political campaigns of China's current ruler, Xi Jinping. This process of undermining foreign companies will eventually work to the detriment of China, but these businesses will be wounded, some grievously.

The discriminatory treatment of foreign companies is bound to get worse over time, complicating already deteriorating relations between Washington and Beijing. There are many grievances that American companies have in China, and the obviously unfair application of the competition laws, the topic of the moment, illustrates important themes common to most of them.

The leaders of the People's Republic have always exhibited some hostility toward foreign companies, but the campaign to undermine them became especially apparent during the rule of Hu Jintao, who stepped down as Communist Party general secretary in November 2012. During his tenure, officials cited various concerns, including those relating to competition, to block high-profile foreign acquisitions, especially beginning in 2007 with Microsoft's attempt to take a stake in Sichuan Changhong Electric and Goldman Sachs's moves on Midea Electric and Fuyao Group. Carlyle Group, the investment firm, at around that time was frustrated in its long pursuit of Xugong Group Construction Machinery.

Anti-Monopoly Law

Beijing's efforts really got into high gear, however, when the Anti-Monopoly Law came into effect in 2008. The central government didn't waste time using its new club, stopping Coca-Cola from buying Huiyuan Juice Group in 2009.

China's campaign escalated still further in July of last year. Then, the powerful National Development and Reform Commission brought together representatives from about 30 foreign companies—including Microsoft, GE, IBM, Intel, and Qualcomm—and tried to force them to write confessions of violations of the Anti-Monopoly Law. Chinese officials, incredibly, showed the multinationals the "self-criticisms" of other companies as a means of pressuring them to follow suit.

NDRC officials, during the two-day meeting, also browbeat and threatened the foreign firms and warned them not to defend themselves. "The message was: if you put up a fight, I could double or triple your fines," said one participant at the session, reporting the remarks of the NDRC's Xu Xinyu, a division chief in the antitrust bureau.

Since then, Beijing has gone after one multinational after another. Recent American targets include Chrysler, fined last week, and General Motors. Moreover, regulators have investigated non-American firms as well. The offensive against foreign companies of all stripes has become so notorious that it has become a part of the global discourse. *Time* at the end of July asked this: "Is no famous foreign brand safe in China?"

With the Chinese government going on an unmistakable anti-foreign bender, the answer to *Time*'s question is obviously no. China's most egregious anti-trust violators are its large state enterprises, but they have escaped the attention of the NDRC and Beijing's two other competition enforcers, the State Administration for Industry and Commerce and the Ministry of Commerce. And that uneven focus raises concerns Beijing is openly violating its World Trade Organization obligations, especially its promise to provide "national treatment"—nondiscriminatory administration of its laws—to foreign companies. These days, arrogant Chinese officials are making less and less pretense of honoring international trade obligations.

"Xi's 'China Dream' has become 'China First,' " writes Richard Harris of Port Shelter Investment Management, referring to the signature campaign of Xi Jinping. "But for now the strategy is to keep tilting the playing field in your favor until someone notices."

Now, many are noticing. In the past month, the U.S. Chamber of Commerce, the American Chamber of Commerce in China, the U.S.-China Business Council, and the European Union Chamber of Commerce have issued reports complaining of discriminatory treatment and intimidation in connection with the Anti-Monopoly Law. Moreover, the U.S. government has begun to take an interest. On the 10th of this month, for instance, Edith Ramirez, chairwoman of the U.S. Federal Trade Commission, voiced concerns about Beijing's move against Qualcomm. On the 14th, the *Wall Street Journal* reported that Treasury Secretary Jacob Lew had written to Vice Premier Wang Yang about the anti-monopoly investigations.

The Chinese government has now felt compelled to answer critics. On the 9th of this month, Chinese Premier Li Keqiang told business executives that his government ran anti-monopoly investigations "legally, transparently and fairly," and two days later China's three anti-monopoly regulators banded together to defend their conduct at an unusual joint press conference. "Our anti-trust enforcement work is strictly conducted according to regulations," said the NDRC's Xu Kunlin of the Price Supervision and Inspection and Anti-Monopoly Bureau. "It is fair and transparent. It is not targeting any market player, and of course, it is not targeting any foreign invested or foreign enterprise."

No one believes the blanket denials, but many now hope China will stop persecuting American and other multinationals. Will Beijing relent? Analysts ascribe Beijing's blatantly discriminatory treatment to temporary or non-structural factors.

First, many say the campaign against foreign companies is largely a squabble about market share, that increasingly powerful state enterprises are using their political clout to take business opportunities from these successful outside competitors. Beijing, after all, has been going after Microsoft's competitive practices—and banning Windows 8 this year as well as attacking its OneDrive cloud storage service—in anticipation of the central government's attempt to introduce its own operating system, perhaps as early as this year.

Second, some argue that anti-foreign enforcement will essentially end when the campaign hits China in the pocketbook. Foreign direct investment plunged 17.0% in July from the same month in 2013 and was down 0.35% for the first seven months of this year from the corresponding period in 2013. Many attribute the fall partly to Beijing's unwelcoming attitude to foreign business, and a few think Chinese bureaucrats will let up on anti-monopoly investigations to stem the downturn in FDI.

Third, there are indications that Chinese leaders are targeting foreign business as the economy continues to slide, and many analysts see it reviving later. The National Bureau of Statistics claims growth around 7.5%, but independent data, private surveys, and even government numbers indicate the economy stumbling badly, with growth already in the low single digits. Foreign companies would make the perfect villain if growth disappears, as it may by the end of this year.

There is truth in all of these contentions, but there are powerful factors suggesting that the long-term effort against foreign companies will continue because it is rooted in the country's corrosive politics.

Fundamental Political Problem

Communist Party politics will likely remain unfavorable to multinationals for the long term. The campaign against them is almost certainly directed from the top of the Chinese political system, the Party's seven-member Politburo Standing Committee, because nothing this important could be maintained without approval from the highest levels of the one-party state.

That approval is evidenced by both the length of the campaign—going back more than a half decade—and the breath of the effort. While Beijing goes after multinationals for violations of competition law, it has also been harassing them in other ways, such as its highly discriminatory enforcement of bribery laws, most noticeable in the pharmaceutical sector. This is, for instance, more than just a squabble about the market share of state enterprises.

Unfortunately, the frontal attack on foreign business brings to mind the xenophobia of Mao's era. Xi Jinping has been conducting a series of Maoist-inspired "rectification" and "mass line" campaigns since he took over as China's leader. The use of Cultural Revolution-style methods against multinationals suggests that his Maoist rhetoric is already affecting Chinese governance.

Worse, Xi is now taking the country backward in another important respect. China prospered when it opened up its economy after the horrible Maoist years. Now, however, he is reversing course. He talks positive change but has, on important matters, sponsored regressive economic moves. Whether or not Xi has abandoned Deng Xiaoping's transformational policies—encapsulated by the phrase "reform and opening up"—he is on balance moving China's economy in an unproductive direction.

As Arthur Waldron of the University of Pennsylvania points out, the Chinese are often thought of as pragmatists but at this moment their leaders are not acting pragmatically. There are many reasons why this is so, but the most important of them relates to the nature of the Chinese system. As James Zimmerman, former chairman of the American Chamber of Commerce in China, points out, "Despite all of the reform and progress to date, China is still a command economy driven by a political agenda that seeks to first and foremost legitimize the party in power."

Xi Jinping is trying to legitimize the Communist Party by attacking foreigners. The narrative is that they charge too much for their goods and services in the country, so Xi is using coercive tactics to make them reduce prices. It does not matter that their prices are high largely because of the Party's abnormal economic system; Microsoft and others make perfect targets.

So political incentives are pushing Chinese officials to go after foreigners. In all likelihood, the seemingly unrelenting campaign is bound to intensify, if not in the months ahead then at least in the longer term. As Zimmerman suggests, the fault is in the nature of China's one-party state, something that no Chinese leader is willing to change.

Foreign business has to be concerned that political turmoil will worsen in coming months. Although most analysts believe Xi Jinping consolidated power quickly, there are more and more signs of disunity in senior Party circles. For instance, the continual purges and loyalty oaths are indications of substantial resistance to his rule and dissension at the top. And Xi's own words of being stalemated, reportedly uttered at a June 26 Politburo meeting, indicate continued trouble ahead. In this environment, it's not entirely clear that Beijing is able to deal fairly with foreign companies operating on its own soil, whether in the anti-monopoly area or others of contention.

No country today can prosper for long by retreating from the globalized economy. Ultimately, China will be the biggest victim of its hostility to foreign business, but before then multinationals—and especially American ones—will be hurt.

Solutions

It's clear, considering everything, that Xi will not stop the offensive against American multinationals until the costs that the U.S. government imposes on China exceeds the substantial benefits it derives from disadvantaging them.

Treasury Secretary Lew's letter to Beijing warned that discriminatory treatment could have, in the words of the *Wall Street Journal*, "serious implications for relations between the two countries." Those words are a step in the right direction, but they have to be backed up by action if Chinese authorities do not relent. Washington in the past has been loath to impose real costs on China, and Beijing surely senses that reluctance.

With China's growing reliance on exports, Washington has the leverage to stop Beijing in its tracks. For instance, last year the country's merchandise trade surplus against America was a record $318.7 billion, a stunning 122.7% of its overall merchandise surplus. We can find other locations to manufacture goods—a process that is already occurring—but Beijing cannot find other markets.

We can protect our companies by limiting China's access to our market through special tariffs and other mechanisms. The only question is whether the U.S. government has the will to do so.

Mr. CHABOT. Thank you very much. Really excellent testimony. We were both just commenting on that. Very, very good. I will recognize myself for the purpose of asking questions for 5 minutes.

Let me begin with you, Mr. Johnson. Since President Xi assumed power, it seems that we have seen a discernible change in China's behavior. It is more aggressive, more risk oriented and it seems pretty much impervious to U.S. pressure. As today's hearing title suggests, it seems we are entering a new era in U.S.-China relations. First, would you agree? And second, how can the administration recalibrate its strategy to more effectively deal with China's fundamentally different approach to foreign and economic policies?

Mr. JOHNSON. Thank you, Mr. Chairman. It is my perception that indeed we are entering a fundamentally different period under Xi Jinping's leadership with regard to his approach to Sino-U.S. relations but also to China's foreign policy at large, and I think there are several reasons for that.

The first is that unlike his most immediate predecessor, Hu Jintao, Xi Jinping is a very confident leader, someone who does command the system, has a deep political network that runs throughout the system, and has very strong views about how he thinks about China's place in the world. It was very telling, for example, when he was first revealed as the new leader of China. In his opening speech, which was very brief, he put a lot of emphasis on these concepts of the Chinese dream and the great rejuvenation of the Chinese people and China as a nation. And I think we see this stream running through his foreign policy approach.

With regard to the U.S., I think the fundamental thing to understand in terms of how Xi Jinping approaches the relationship is that unlike his two predecessors who arguably spent between 80 and 90 percent of their foreign policy energy, or bandwidth, if you will, focused on Sino-U.S. relations whether those relations were good, bad or indifferent.

Xi Jinping does not operate that way. His view is that he does not, of course he is not seeking to sort of diminish the status of U.S.-China relations, but he is not as solicitous or desirous of the relationship as his predecessors have been. And I think we have seen that time and again.

So for as just one example, you had the Sunnylands meeting between our two leaders. Things seemed very solid in that meeting and a good opportunity for the two Presidents to be able to get to know each other and to think about how we might indeed go through this new style of major country relations. But since then we have seen this drift come in and traditional mechanisms like the Strategic and Economic Dialogue between our two countries, which in my assessment has become a fairly useless entity, we are not connecting on this level. And I think it is because when President Xi looks at President Obama he sees a leader who unlike himself is not confident, is not control of his own system, is not reliable.

And in the long management of U.S.-China relations, the most important thing to the Chinese side is consistency. They will take a difficult position from the United States when necessary if they know that the leader is consistent, and they have real questions about the consistency in President Obama's approach.

In terms of his broader foreign policy strategy and the things you mentioned with regard to his approach to the neighbors, what we see, I think, is a fundamental rejection, if you will, by Xi Jinping of the longstanding foreign policy dictum stated by Deng Xiaoping, which is that China should bide its time, keep a low profile, never take the lead internationally.

It was very telling to me that when the Foreign Minister Wang Yi gave his first press conference in the spring at their national legislative session, when asked by the CCTV reporter in the audience, so obviously a planted question, how would you describe the success of China's foreign policy under the new leadership in the first year in office, he said, in a word, active, which tells us a lot. Because 35 years ago, no senior Chinese official would have described their foreign policy as active.

So how should the U.S. respond to——

Mr. CHABOT. Can I cut you off here?

Mr. JOHNSON. Sure. Yes.

Mr. CHABOT. Because I am almost out of time and I think Mr. Chang should respond to that question as well for a minute or two.

Mr. CHANG. I think that when Xi Jinping looks at Obama and Obama looks at Xi Jinping, he must think that the Chinese leader himself is unreliable, and the problem is of distress in the political system. June 26, Politburo meeting, Xi Jinping admits that his signature campaign against corruption, which is really just a political purge, was stalemated. And then he talked in melodramatic terms about his own death.

Well, there have a been a number of coup rumors over the last 3 years, some of very recent vintage. We don't know a lot of what is going on, but we can see that there are things which are not consistent with a stable political system in China. So that I think is going to be driving U.S.-China relations.

Mr. CHABOT. Okay, thank you very much. My time has expired, and I will recognize the ranking member, Mr. Faleomavaega.

Mr. FALEOMAVAEGA. Thank you, Mr. Chairman. To counter the U.S. pivot to Asia, China is aggressively pushing for free trade agreements within the Asia-Pacific region which include South Korea and Japan, and looking somewhat of a maritime Silk Road, if you will, it will also create free trade agreements with Southeast Asian countries.

I would like to ask both gentlemen of what significant impact will this have on the United States especially within the administration's ongoing efforts with the Trans-Pacific Partnership initiative?

Mr. CHANG. Obviously I think there is going to be competition between the United States and China. China's trade with the region certainly has grown dramatically with all of its neighbors, but I think that to a certain extent we are seeing troubles in the Chinese economy itself. It is not growing at the 7.5 percent that Beijing claims. It is probably closer to 1 or 2 percent.

And I think that we are going to see a decrease and a decline in Chinese trade with its neighbors despite all of these free trade agreements. The Trans-Pacific Partnership concept is very important for the United States because when we talk about the pivot we often think about military means, but really the most important part of the pivot is the Trans-Pacific Partnership because that will be there for generations.

Mr. FALEOMAVAEGA. Mr. Johnson?

Mr. JOHNSON. I would just add briefly to that by saying that the TPP really is the fulcrum of the rebalance in the region. And in the Asia-Pacific region, economics is security. That is how the countries in the region view it. And so without TPP there is no economic counterweight to what China has been doing, and then this often will end up driving some of their behavior toward the Philippines, toward Vietnam.

I think the assessment sometimes in Beijing is, why shouldn't be assertive with this when ultimately these countries will have to knuckle under because of their economic dependence on China? Likewise, I think it is the best way that we can signal to the region that there is truth, there is action behind our rhetoric with regard to our statements about being in the region for the long term.

Mr. FALEOMAVAEGA. There are at least 11 independent Pacific Islands nations, each have a vote in the United Nations. It is no secret that China, in 2009 alone, gave over $200 million in aid to these Pacific Island countries. Is there a connection between the U.N. votes and the increased aid, and, if so, does this pose a security threat to our interests, Australia, as well as New Zealand?

Mr. CHANG. I believe there are 14 U.N. votes in the Pacific, and this is, I think, one of the important things for China. Clearly it was important for China's initiatives toward Africa and Latin America. And to the extent that the U.N. is relevant and that changes day by day, then of course this is going to be important because the U.S. will be outvoted in the General Assembly time after time unless we have much better relations with countries in the Pacific.

And one important thing on that is that China's relations, economic relations, are not always to the benefit of those islands and those nations. We need to have better trade. This is something that we can really win.

Mr. FALEOMAVAEGA. Mr. Johnson?

Mr. JOHNSON. Yes, I would agree with that and simply add that this is another area, while not affecting those islands where TPP is so important in terms of getting a U.S. style standard involved in a lot of these free trade agreements, because what we see with the Chinese is a lot of direct buying of influence with these countries through economic projects and so on.

Mr. FALEOMAVAEGA. I don't have the exact geography of the situation in the Pacific region, but I know that the compact of these Pacific Island countries compose at least a vast part of the world's geography as far as sea bed minerals, marine resources. Do you think the United States should pay a little more attention to the situation there in that region?

Mr. JOHNSON. Absolutely.

Mr. FALEOMAVAEGA. Okay. I am sorry, my time is up. Thank you, Mr. Chairman.

Mr. CHABOT. Thank you very much, Mr. Faleomavaega. The gentleman from Calfornia, Mr. Rohrabacher, is recognized for 5 minutes.

Mr. ROHRABACHER. I have often told people who want to invest in other countries and do business and then they come to me and they want different type of trade agreements that would facilitate their commerce in other countries, I always say that I do believe in free trade, but I believe that in free trade between free people. And that when you have a free trade system with a dictatorship or with a country that is run by a clique as we seem to see in China that the trade will be manipulated in order to enrich the clique.

And is what we have is a basically a clique in China that is, I noticed there is so many more millionaires being created. If you are in the clique you have opportunity and freedom, if you are out of the clique the system will work against you? Is that what we face there in China?

Mr. CHANG. That is certainly the case that we face in China. Just today I heard the story of a U.S. investor, Susan Weinstein, whose investment was completely taken away by Shanghai gangsters. So this is the clique at work.

China's trade behavior, since it joined the World Trade Organization at the end of 2001, has deteriorated over the last 3 or 4 years in very ways that are troubling. Because we were always told that China would become a good trader, would become a part of the international system, well, in effect, over the last 3 or 4 years it has gotten much worse, and so therefore there is a problem.

And if I may say so, I think that China's desire, the Communist Party's desire for control, which has manifested itself on these antimonopoly investigations, is the same desire for control of Christians and other people of faith in China.

Mr. ROHRABACHER. I guess you might call this what we are describing as the ultimate crony capitalism, which is, in other words some people believe crony capitalism is actually fascism which is another way of expressing that.

If American companies invest overseas, and now we have this example where foreign companies are being targeted for aggressive legal action, I don't think this should surprise these businessmen. I mean you go and you invest in a country that does not have an independent court system, am I correct in assuming that if there is a business disagreement or if the government has something to do that the court system is not in any way a fair or free court system there?

Mr. CHANG. The last thing that I did, Mr. Rohrabacher, practicing law in Shanghai, was involved in a multiyear case as a representative of a foreign bank against a local company. And the odds were stacked so much against us it was not a fair fight and, accordingly, we ended up on the short side of the stick. But this experience is just replicated thousands of times a year.

Mr. ROHRABACHER. Well, we know that China is not only condoning but, actually, the government of the clique that runs the country is actually participating in the theft of American intellectual property rights and cyberattacks, et cetera.

American businessmen who have been insisting on a free trade approach with this type of country, I hope they don't come to us now pleading with us to help them out. By investing overseas, an American company that invests overseas in order to make a 20 percent profit rather than investing here and making a 10-percent profit have basically betrayed the American people. Working people in our country who go to war, pay their taxes, insist on honest government, and those honest citizens here who expect perhaps those people with more money in our society to take their well being into consideration when making business decisions.

Well, the fact that those companies have gone over there, they are getting their comeuppance and they should have watched out for what we Americans hold dear in the first place and they wouldn't be so vulnerable. So I would suggest, Mr. Chairman, that we not go out of our way to protect the American companies that are now in jeopardy in China.

Mr. CHABOT. Thank you very much. The gentleman yields back. The gentleman also from California, Mr. Bera, is recognized for 5 minutes.

Mr. BERA. Thank you, Mr. Chairman. Thanks for calling this incredibly important hearing. From what both the witnesses have described, China clearly is at a crossroads and over the past few years it has been at a political crossroads, an economic crossroads. Yet, China's importance to the region in terms of trade with regional partners, Japan, Korea, the Southeast Asian nations, and obviously the importance of being a trading partner with us also has grown.

China has to make some decisions now. And I think Mr. Chang you touched on one of the leverage points that we have. Because of China's dependence on exports and their dependence on exports to the United States, yes, there probably are opportunities for us to leverage that reliance on exporting to us.

So one of my questions, and then one of my thoughts and then I would let the comment here, within this committee we have looked at North Korea and some of the challenges that we face in North Korea and the importance of needing a regional approach and China's importance in leveraging North Korea to become a more responsible player in the world.

How would, just again thinking, through knowing that you have written a book on North Korea as well, how we could leverage that again China has to be an important partner as we approach North Korea, and approach it not as a U.S. versus North Korea, but the United States with Japan, with Korea, with China, with Russia, to leverage on North Korea?

Mr. CHANG. Historically, China has had the most influence in North Korea, but in recent years, especially the last year, China has had less influence in North Korea than us. And so therefore I don't think we need the Chinese to implement our policies toward Pyongyang. It is a very much of a change of attitude on the Kim regime, but clearly relations between Beijing and Pyongyang have broken down. The United States can act on its own in this case.

Mr. BERA. Should China though be a partner in this at all? Do you think they can be a partner?

Mr. CHANG. We have tried that approach for a decade and didn't work. I don't know if it is going to work now, especially with the problems inside Beijing.

Mr. BERA. Okay.

Mr. JOHNSON. My personal view is that there is more opportunity with the Chinese than there has been in many, many years with regard to North Korea. We have seen that Xi Jinping has taken a somewhat different approach. There has been a lot of commentary in air and ink spilled about whether or not China has changed its policy. Fundamentally it hasn't. It is still what keeps the North Koreans going on a day-to-day basis.

But what we do see is, as Gordon just suggested, a sort of fundamental difference of opinion now between the two leaderships. The one thing that frankly where roping them in as a partner is an important piece, is that they are very much embarked on a campaign now of seeking to peel South Korea off from the alliance with the U.S. and Japan. And we saw this most recently with Xi Jinping's visit to South Korea earlier in the year.

And this is something that we the United States need to be very mindful of and think about how we can leverage not only our relationship with South Korea, but also Chinese concerns about North Korea to try to manage that process.

Mr. BERA. If we shift now to some of the tensions that occurring based on Chinese actions in the East China Sea and the South China Sea and some of the unilaterally provocative moves raising tensions between China and Vietnam in very important trading routes, and then the same thing with the Senkaku Islands in raising tensions between Japan and China, and then obviously the ADIZ unilateral expansions. Again I think all of our regional allies are looking for the United States to make sure we are standing strong there and sending a very strong message.

And I would be curious again how we push back. Because again if these unilateral decisions that China is making go unchecked, they have somewhat of a propensity to continue moving the ball down the field.

So Mr. Johnson?

Mr. JOHNSON. Yes. It is, in fact, one of the things that is maddening about some of these moves that the Chinese are making is that they are very hard to counter in a sophisticated way. One of the challenges is that I believe the Chinese have made the assessment that with regard to how to manage these kind of salami-slicing tactics that we have been seeing from them, they understand that the U.S. tool kit is actually fairly limited. We have rhetorical responses which we have been using, and we have the 7th Fleet. And between there is not a whole lot that we can be doing.

One area though is in the space of improving maritime domain awareness for the littoral countries. This is inexpensive from a U.S. point of view and also will help create a more common picture and understanding of what the Chinese are doing with regard to their reclamation of these atolls and so on.

Mr. BERA. All right. And I think I am out of time.

Mr. CHABOT. Thank you. The gentleman's time has expired. The gentleman from Arizona, Mr. Salmon, is recognized, who is also the subcommittee chairman for the Western Hemisphere.

Mr. SALMON. Thank you very much. And what is really fascinating is that I do not speak Spanish and I am the chairman over the Western Hemisphere. I actually speak Mandarin Chinese, and it doesn't go very far when I go to Mexico.

But anyway this is my second stint in Congress. I was here, in fact, Mr. Chabot and I were elected the same term, 1994——

Mr. CHABOT. Twenty years ago.

Mr. SALMON [continuing]. During the great Contract with America. And I came at a time when every summer we would have a debate on Jackson-Vanik and we would be kicking the stuffings out of China every July. And I became a very strong advocate of PNTR, and I became a very strong advocate of them entering into the WTO.

I was in Seattle at the time a lot of that was happening when they were throwing the chairs through the windows, and I was there at that time. I had been over to China probably over 40 times, and many of those visits I have stayed for as long as a couple of months so I know a little bit about China. I couldn't be more profoundly disappointed in the predictions that I made if China was to get PNTR as far as being a good trader and our values maybe rubbing off on them.

I remember making the argument, I think the most valuable export that we have to China is not to any of the commodities or services but it is our ideals and it is freedom. And I believed at that time that a lot of the human rights issues would become better, that religious freedom would improve.

And I am sad to say that was over a decade ago and it has not. And in many ways, Mr. Johnson, you said it is worse, and I agree. And I think the aggression has become worse. Now our President at the first of this year said that he and his administration would make a pivot to Asia. How is that working out? Is the pivot being made?

Mr. JOHNSON. Well, certainly in terms of the rhetorical pieces of the pivot we have had some execution, but I can tell you that when I travel to the region I am constantly asked by our regional partners and allies, when is it going to materialize? When are we going to see some——

Mr. SALMON. That is what I am wondering too.

Mr. JOHNSON [continuing]. Meat on the bone, if you will——

Mr. SALMON. Yes.

Mr. JOHNSON [continuing]. With regard to how it works. And as I mentioned just a moment ago, things like focusing on building this maritime domain awareness net, enhanced intelligence cooperation, for example, with allies and partners in the region, these are real things that we can be doing with our partners that we aren't, to make this pivot real.

I also would just underscore again what both Gordon and I suggested with regard to TPP and the importance of that in terms of balancing the rebalance, right?

Mr. SALMON. Well, right after the President spoke in his State of the Union and said that TPA and TPP were extremely important, the majority leader on the other side said, over my dead body. And there has been, really, no push from the administration to move over that.

Mr. JOHNSON. Well, this is a fundamental challenge. I mean I have yet to see a legislative strategy from the administration——

Mr. SALMON. Exactly.

Mr. JOHNSON [continuing]. In moving TPP forward.

Mr. SALMON. And it is very, very frustrating. I have a specific question. Because when I left in my private life, one of the things I did was I became the CEO of a company that was manufacturing its product over in China and it actually had patents all over the world filed.

And we had a really interesting phenomenon happen in China, and that was that when we filed our patent in China we had some bad actor cross file, and then what he did because the courts were colluding with him, what he basically wanted was extortion money. Buy him off for several million dollars so that he would go away. Do you see a lot of that?

Mr. JOHNSON. Constantly. And this is one area where, the main problem in these litigations is that the local court is appointed, paid and overseen by the local party, provincial administration. And if the key SOE in the province is the one you are up against, guess who is going to win the court case? It happens this way every time.

And so this is something where we are watching carefully. They will have their plenum here in a couple weeks. The official theme is supposed to be Rule By Law, so it will be——

Mr. SALMON. And while the central government has passed some very robust laws regarding IP violations, the problem is there is no enforcement.

Mr. JOHNSON. Local enforcement, yes.

Mr. SALMON. There is no enforcement. And when you get down to the provincial levels, they are doing their own thing and they don't answer to the Federal Government, and so, really, nothing has really changed. In fact, it is as bad as it has ever been. Is that correct?

Mr. JOHNSON. That is my assessment.

Mr. SALMON. What would you say, Mr. Chang?

Mr. CHANG. That is certainly correct. And it is because there is, the Chinese central government if it wants to do something it can find Falun Gong practitioners in some upland——

Mr. SALMON. Exactly.

Mr. CHANG [continuing]. Remote place thousands of miles from Beijing, but it can't enforce patent infringements in Beijing. If I just may so, I think that American trade has affected the Chinese people. The Chinese people now think very much the way we do on the issues that you talk about, it is just that the Chinese political system has gone the other way. And so that is, I think, the paradox.

Mr. SALMON. Thank you. I am out of time. Would love to talk with you a lot more. It is good stuff.

Mr. CHANG. Thank you.

Mr. CHABOT. The gentleman's time has expired. Is the gentleman ready? We are doing a second round and we will start with Mr. Sherman.

Mr. SHERMAN. Only in America would we ignore this enormous trade deficit and focus instead on whether the Japanese get a few islands, excuse me, rocks that we mischaracterize as islands.

I don't know if either of you can answer this. Why is that Germany is able to run a trade surplus with China, whereas we run the world's, the largest trade deficit in the history of mammalian life?

Mr. JOHNSON. I am going to largely defer to Gordon on this one, but I would simply suggest that it is because the Germans still make things. But——

Mr. CHANG. I would like to defer to Mr. Johnson, but since he has already started, I think that the most important thing is that the United States has become strong by having open markets.

Mr. SHERMAN. No, the United States has become weak by having open markets. You are not in touch with the working and middle class families that have been decimated while the grad school educated elite in the country does so well. This has not been a period of strength for America. This has been a period of decimation for our families.

So you can continue.

Mr. CHANG. The problem is that China has become much more mercantilist as I mentioned before and trade behavior has deteriorated. And it is a paradox for the United States because it is a very difficult problem in that the sense that we do believe in open markets and yet you have a predatory trader.

And the question is, how do you deal with that one trader while still keeping the markets open which we believe to be important? And it is, I think, because there has been ineffective enforcement on the part of various administrations to Chinese behavior, because we have always thought they would get better. But over the last 3 or 4 years they have gotten worse. And so I think that we need to actually start to look at some much more punitive measures to make sure that as I said before that we impose costs that are greater on them than the benefits that they get by being mercantilists.

Mr. SHERMAN. Well, I think you misunderstand the gravity of the situation. Every year they become another $300 billion richer and we lose 2 million to 3 million jobs.

Japan is happy to have us expand our military spending to defend islets that they hope will have oil which they will not share with us. And of course they exaggerate the importance of these. What is the Japanese military expenditure as a percentage of their GDP?

Mr. CHANG. One percent, I believe.

Mr. SHERMAN. I believe it is way less than 1 percent, isn't it? Isn't 1 percent a ceiling they aspire to?

Mr. CHANG. You very well may be——

Mr. SHERMAN. So now these same families that have been decimated should pay higher taxes to the Federal Government so that we can make sure to have a strong naval presence to defend the oil that doesn't exist which will accrue to a nation that isn't willing to spend its own money. We have decided to be hawks on Japanese rocks and doves on trade. This meets the institutional needs of Washington and the Pentagon and Wall Street, and obviously is part of an overall program that has decimated American working families.

I will yield back in hopes of an interesting second round.

Mr. CHABOT. Okay, the gentleman yields back.

Let me start with you if I can, Mr. Chang. You had mentioned the $318 billion deficit that we have with China, and I think I share a lot of concerns with Mr. Salmon, because we supported, what was at that time PNTR, which then became normal trade relations and other things. What can we really do? If you were King, what would you do to deal directly with that $318 billion trade deficit that we have with China?

Mr. CHANG. Well, the one thing that I would do is I would get on the phone with Xi Jinping and say that if he didn't stop XY and Z that essentially the U.S. would start inspecting goods at the Port of Long Beach. And that way the container ships would be lined halfway across the Pacific.

And I know that some people believe that rigorous inspection of Customs is a WTO violation, but nonetheless, these guys play very hard and I think that we should play as hard with them as they play with us. We have to remember that the Blair-Huntsman Commission talked about a special tariff because of Chinese intellectual property violations. And indeed a special tariff, I think, would be something that could work in a number of different areas, and so therefore it is one of the things that we should look at.

But as long as we only talk about these things and don't actually impose costs, we will never have any progress with the Chinese on trade issues.

Mr. CHABOT. Thank you. You mentioned that you would say unless he does XY and Z that we are going to do these things. What would X or Y or Z be? What are the things that we really ought to demand from him?

Mr. CHANG. Well, I think the thing that is most important would be the subsidies that China gives to its manufacturers to give them an extraordinary advantage, not only in global markets but in China's own market of course. The list changes day by day. I mean 1 year ago we would not have been talking so much about the antimonopoly investigations, but now of course they are the topic du jour.

This list is going to change, but the list is comprehensive and we could come up in short order with a list of about 30 things that need to be done. And I would be happy to do that for the committee if they so request.

Mr. CHABOT. All right, well, thank you. I think we will request that. So we appreciate that very much.

Let me ask both of you this. You suggested one method to mitigate the Chinese offensive against American companies is for companies finding other locations to manufacture their goods, and that is going to take some time for that to happen. You referred to it as a frontal attack on foreign businesses. At what point do the foreign businesses either realize this or does it no longer become, maybe not unprofitable, but not profitable enough to take all this grief from China? Are we approaching that point or did they make enough money now that they are willing to put up with the garbage that they are putting up with?

So either one of you or both of you.

Mr. JOHNSON. I will just offer a couple brief remarks. I think that what we can say is that American firms, European firms, other firms operating in the country certainly have noticed that the environment has become much more difficult. I think it is fair to say that 5 years ago when firms were considering an investment in China, the discussion at the board level was rather simpler. It is China, it is huge, we have to be there, go.

Now I think firms are taking the opportunity to think more deliberately about what might we get out of this particular investment? What type of return might we be able to receive? What will we give away both voluntarily and involuntarily through cyber and other issues that we worry about? And are we in an industry that it would actually make sense for us to be operating in this current China landscape that they face?

Mr. CHABOT. Thank you. Let me ask you this, Mr. Chang, because I have only 1 minute to go. You mentioned when the Chinese Government pulled these 20 American corporations, I think?

Mr. CHANG. There were 30, and they were mostly American but there were others as well.

Mr. CHABOT. All right. So could you tell us a little more about that? What happened, where was it at and what were they demanding of these people?

Mr. CHANG. There were two series of meetings. There was one set of meetings for Chinese companies. There was another set of meetings for foreign companies. Both sets of meetings were conducted in Chinese so there was no need to have two sets of meetings. And, essentially, over 2 days, what the NDRC, the National Development and Reform Commission, did was wanting to force them to write confessions and essentially to agree to fines for violations of the antimonopoly law, and companies of course resisted.

To answer your other point, foreign direct investment is starting to fall in China. In July it was down 17.0 percent. I forget the figure for August. But it is not only the falls in July and August, but also for 2014 as a whole FDI is down. This is the first time this has occurred since China joined the WTO in 2001.

Mr. CHABOT. I am out of time, but do the Chinese realize that this could have the opposite effect that they desire? That they may end up shooting themselves in the foot?

Mr. CHANG. I think they do realize that, but I also think that they can't do very much about it because of Chinese state-owned enterprises being too powerful within the Chinese system. And so I think senior leaders, like Li Keqiang, the Premier of China, can talk about this issue but there is very little he can actually do about it.

Mr. CHABOT. Thank you very much. My time has expired. Mr. Faleomavaega is recognized for 5 minutes.

Mr. FALEOMAVAEGA. Thank you, Mr. Chairman. I am trying to think in terms of some of the questions and issues that were raised in our hearing this afternoon. It took American democracy over 200 years to develop where we are now, and I was wondering that there is an American Indian saying, walk in a man's moccasins before you make judgment.

China has 1.5 billion people. It is one of the two most populous nations in the world. And even India, if you talk about it, there are tremendous opportunities as well as responsibility. How do you go about in getting a system of government that will address the means or the issues of some 1.5 billion people, not million, billion?

And I want to raise this issue with both of you gentlemen. If you were in the President of China's seat, what would you be doing or saying to provide, to feed 1.5 billion people? Now I know that it seems that our whole interest it seems to be emphasized on strategic and military, but what about considering the social issues that the Chinese people and their leaders have to confront? What do they have to do in order to survive?

It is very easy for us because we are the most powerful, we have the biggest economy in all of this, but it took us 200 years to get where we are now. So I would be happy to hear your comments on that concern.

Mr. CHANG. Well, China took 5,000 years and is still working at it. If I were Xi Jinping, I would think that the Communist Party system has basically run to its limits. It is very much, it cannot really progress very much further within the authoritarian system. And I would open it up for elections. I would have very much fewer regulations on business. I would get the state of business by privatizing state-owned enterprises.

But fortunately or unfortunately I am not the leader of China, and he is absolutely resistant to all the things that I just talked about.

Mr. JOHNSON. I would simply add that this is probably the core challenge that the Communist Party leadership faces going forward. You have a very stovepiped and rickety Leninist system riding atop one of the world's most dynamic countries and whether or not the Party leadership can reinvent themselves in some way.

And I really think it speaks very much to what Mr. Chang just said with regard to we are not going to see the type of reform and progress we want to see until the Party is able to step back from the economy, and so far that is just something they have not been willing to do.

Mr. FALEOMAVAEGA. How would you then compare the socio-economic interests of the Soviet Union, or what we now call Russia, in terms of the development that they have taken? Is it more a free market oriented or are they still having problems with Lenin and the ideologies involved in that?

Mr. JOHNSON. They don't have troubles with Lenin, they have troubles with mafias. It is an even more crony capitalistic system than that you might see in China.

Mr. FALEOMAVAEGA. Mr. Chang?

Mr. CHANG. What we see in both places was the Soviet Union looked to be more vibrant than it actually was. I think China is less vibrant than it appears to be. China's problem right now is that it has run up enormous amounts of debt. It has put in enormous amounts of stimulus since the end of 2008 to avoid the effects of the global downturn. And so it does have critical threats to its economy, but they are very different than the ones that faced the Soviet Union at the end.

So essentially you have a political system that is dominating the economy that is not allowing the actors in the economy to do what is absolutely necessary to create sustainable prosperity.

Mr. FALEOMAVAEGA. Two of the most populous nations in the world are side by side, and I am talking about India and China. And there seems to be a development ongoing in trying to figure how they can provide programs that will naturally benefit them economically. Do you think the United States should have a policy in promoting better economic relations with China as well?

Mr. CHANG. I think that we should have a policy which is much more focused on India. It is a democracy. We share values with them. We also face a belligerence of China and so we do face common threats. But I think the most important thing is values and then that will create a stable relationship. The United States has not had a stable relationship with a large authoritarian nation ever, and I don't think that what we are trying to do now is capable of success.

Mr. FALEOMAVAEGA. Mr. Johnson?

Mr. JOHNSON. I would note that what is interesting, especially with now that Mr. Modi is in as Prime Minister of India, certainly, and has a track record of holding very strong and negative views about China, but yet we see that the two leaderships are trying to court each other in this early process.

I would simply emphasize that for the United States, the main thing for us to remember is India will never agree to be part of some sort of pincer movement to surround China. The economic relationship is too strong. And so we have to be mindful of the limits of how we might be able to——

Mr. FALEOMAVAEGA. Thank you, Mr. Chairman.

Mr. CHABOT. The gentleman's time has expired. The gentleman from Virginia, Mr. Connolly, is recognized for 5 minutes.

Mr. CONNOLLY. Thank you, Mr. Chairman, and I have an opening statement I would ask be entered in the record.

Mr. CHABOT. Without objection, so ordered.

Mr. CONNOLLY. I thank the chair.

Mr. Chang, I would like to pick up on something that just intrigued me the way you put it. That China's Communist system, Communist political apparatus, has maybe kind of run the clock. I mean it is time out. It is over. I wonder if you could go into that just a little bit more, because two things strike me about China. One is, there is a sense, almost an obsessive sense of the need for order, and order historically flows from Beijing. And they have good reason given just 20th century history why one might abhor the opposite of order, the chaos of revolution and individual militias and of course the Japanese occupation and then the virtual civil war between the Kuomintang and the Communists led by Mao.

So does that, if I am right about almost, well, an obsessive concern about order given their history, does that not give the Communist Party some more rationale on staying power than otherwise might exist in other countries where Communism, in fact, govern?

Mr. CHANG. I think that a desire for order gives a government strength, but only up to a point and they have passed that point. What is important right now is that the Communist Party no longer inspires the Chinese people, and the increasing expenditure on internal security, I think, is a symptom of decline.

The other reason why the Chinese Communist Party has run out the clock is essentially economic. What they have done is they have created massive amounts of debt, perhaps as much as between 15 to 30 percent a year increase in debt over the last 5 years, and they have not been able to create growth that is sufficient to pay back that debt.

So China is on the edge of a debt crisis, plus also a property meltdown which is what we are seeing at this present moment as property markets across the country decline. So essentially the problem is fundamentally economic, but it underlines a political problem of not being able to inspire the Chinese people.

Mr. CONNOLLY. Did you want to comment? You were shaking your head, Mr. Johnson.

Mr. JOHNSON. I take a somewhat different view. My own view is that the Communist Party in China has proven itself to be a very flexible and resilient entity. And that while they do face a lot of these challenges, one thing that distinguishes them from some of the other Communist systems, especially the Soviet Union, that have existed is that they are far more aware about the problems going on inside the country than their Soviet counterpart was. They are far more aware of that.

And we see them historically being willing to take very pragmatic steps to keep the wheel turning. I do think there is a question under whether this new leadership under Xi Jinping where he has really emphasized control and almost a sort of looking back toward an earlier era of ideological indoctrination, whether or not that is the right course for them to be taking.

Mr. CONNOLLY. But I think implicit in Mr. Chang's observation is the fact that perhaps in a high tech, knowledge based economy you have got to have unclad, unfettered ideas, unfettered expression of ideas, unfettered exchange of ideas.

Mr. JOHNSON. Correct.

Mr. CONNOLLY. And that is antithetical to any authoritarian system, especially a Communist system. And so buried in his comment, I think, is a prediction that even if you don't agree that the Communist system is rickety, corrupt and lacking in legitimacy, increasingly, nonetheless the driver of a contemporary economy is just running headlong into that structure and one or the other has to give.

Mr. JOHNSON. Yes. Precisely so. I mean this is one of the challenges they are facing now, right, is their problem with innovation. And I would like to remind Chinese friends that for 5,000 years of their history they didn't have a problem with innovation and then the Communist Party took over and suddenly they have had some difficulty with it.

Unfortunately the practical ramification of that, I would argue, is that they know that in order to solve a lot of the problems that Mr. Chang has referenced in their economy, they do need to move up that value chain much faster than they previously had assessed. Given the challenges that that system, the restraints that it puts on innovation, unfortunately for things like cyber, I think it sends all of the incentives in the wrong direction and we should plan on seeing it increase.

Mr. CONNOLLY. Yes, good point. Mr. Chang, I invoked your name and characterized your comment. Did you just want to add to that in terms of the knowledge based economy?

Mr. CHANG. The problem is that manufacturing is becoming more expensive in China. They are losing low end manufacturing but they are not able to move up the value chain fast enough to replace what they have lost. And that is going to be the critical dynamic in China's economy going forward.

Mr. CONNOLLY. Thank you. Thank you both. Thank you Mr. Chairman.

Mr. CHABOT. Thank you. The gentleman's time is expired. The gentleman from Georgia, Mr. Collins, is recognized for 5 minutes.

Mr. COLLINS. Thank you, Mr. Chairman. I am not sure what is going on today. It is just a privilege for me to be following my friend from Virginia everywhere, but let him know that I am following him as we go. It is good to be—he can take that and he will understand as it goes, and we have had a good time.

This is a concern, and I agree, I am glad of the hearing here, Mr. Chairman, and I appreciate you calling it. As recently returned from China and speaking to, dealing especially from my position in judiciary and intellectual property and intellectual property courts, we had a lot of good discussions with the intermediate courts in speaking in different areas.

What was amazing to me was is while we were there dealing with antitrust and dealing with these kind of, the monopolistic provisions, all across the front page of the very, I guess, fairly stated propagandistic China Daily, today was the issue of they are going after Mercedes Benz and others and after market parts.

The interesting part was is they were not really attacking, in all fairness, the status of what they have and their market share, what they were trying to do is negotiate price. And this is where, I think, we have got to come back. Because just in a matter of a few days, the companies all lower their prices and is amazingly how it all goes away. So you can't have a monopolistic or antitrust violation that goes away with a price decrease. If that would be, then you would have a lot of different issues in this here.

I think the interesting thing that I love to hear is companies in the competition clauses and other things, and then we can get into trademarks. There is so much from a rich environment here and a judiciary aspect that is costing our companies in—what I thought was very interesting was to hearing from some of them that Wallway and several others were actually moving facilities out of China because they were concerned about their own intellectual properties being taken to other companies and stolen with inside the country, so they were actually moving them off on a quasi-state-owned basis.

So how do we encourage China? And I know probably some of it has been discussed here. This was the part that came across very clear in discussion with the businesses but also with the business community, American business, foreign business community in China and also with the Chinese themselves and the government.

How do we encourage a sped up growth rate, if you would, to be understanding of intellectual property in an international understanding, not just a nationalistic understanding? It is amazing their intellectual property courts are flooded with their own cases. There are very few, actually, from foreign companies.

So I want us a little open ended here for a moment. How do we encourage them to do that in a productive way? How do we encourage them to be a part of this process and give our companies the assurances that when they do go, because they do want to invest over here. We want to have reciprocal investment. How do we do that?

Mr. CHANG. I think that we have tried to do that over the course of about three decades, and virtually everything that we have done has failed. So I don't think that you can do that in a nice way. And as I said, we have to start imposing costs on China because that is the one thing that they do understand.

So unfortunately the engagement process just has seriously failed, and we are seeing that day after day with so many problems not only in the intellectual property area but in the antimonopoly and other areas as well.

Mr. COLLINS. And one of the issues here, I think, that you get into and this is one that we are switching, same gear, is their exchange rate, their monetary system, this is another issue. And just recently if you were just looking, their growth rate is cooling off and they are having trouble sustaining this stimulus based growth and they have actually done a little bit of movement in how they are handling it.

But there are many of us who look at this area in China and think that this is not just a short term problem, when you look at their growth, you look at the empty rates in buildings, these kind of things. Where do you see the next step for them going knowing that they are not going to hit their mark at least realistically but they may artificially try to, how through exchange, through other things, what do you see? Crystal ball it for just a second. What do you see them doing next?

Mr. CHANG. They don't have any solutions. What they did was they poured a massive amount of stimulus into the Chinese economy beginning at the end of 2008. It created growth at first, but now it has created a debt which they can't pay back. They are probably growing now at about 2 percent when you look at independent data, corporate profit results and even official numbers.

So I think they have run out of answers and they know that. And the reason we can see it is that they can't do anything and they haven't done anything in the last year or so. So they are stuck.

Mr. COLLINS. Well, and I think, and not to, inside anything in this, but I think it is also to me looking at it, I think, from a very positive, from a market standpoint, from an American, how we can have a positive relationship here. And as long as we don't turn to a nationalistic interest, which is definitely a concern here, rally the troops, we will go after the Straits, we will do those kind of things, is in looking at how we can continue to have the process of them investing here and we investing in their, and having that mutual exchange where you have a southern part, the Hong Kong, Shenzhen, Guangzhou, those areas down there, the Guangdong province that have basically become a more Western economy and with all that is good and bad about that.

And I think that is going to be an interesting, would be a great time as we continue these hearings, Mr. Chairman. I appreciate your leadership. I appreciate you all being here. We could go for a lot of time but I appreciate your answers.

Thank you. Mr. Chairman, I yield back.

Mr. CHABOT. Thank you very much. The gentleman's time is expired and we will conclude with the gentleman from California, Mr. Sherman.

Mr. SHERMAN. I would like to explore the political vulnerability of the Chinese Government. This is a government which over the last 50 years has provided more economic growth than just about any in world history. They have now turned to nationalism to justify their position. Our institutions in the United States survived the Depression, the Great Recession.

Mr. Johnson, can Beijing survive a recession of the level we placed in 2008 or even the depression that Roosevelt guided us through in the 1930s?

Mr. JOHNSON. I think it is an open question. Certainly what is clear is that they managed to survive the global financial crisis better than a lot of others, but as Mr. Chang said, with serious unintended consequences with regard to their response, and it does speak to the central element which is the state driven system. They poured all this stimulus toward the state banks which gave it to inefficient state-owned enterprises and now they are buried by this level of debt.

I think what we need to see is can the reform program that was tabled at the Party plenum last fall actually be implemented? If it is successful that may be one way that they can deal with such problems going forward and make their system more resilient.

Mr. SHERMAN. Mr. Chang, if this government does lose power, will it just peacefully cede power to a different system? Pull a Gorbachev, shrug your shoulders, walk off the world stage? Or will they use the People's Liberation Army and perhaps even their nuclear weapons in an effort to hold onto their system?

Mr. CHANG. I think that when China goes, and it will go fairly soon, it will be pretty ugly. You have got to remember that the Chinese Communist Party——

Mr. SHERMAN. Nuclear ugly or one step less than that?

Mr. CHANG. Ugly with regard to its own people. And what we could also see is China doing——

Mr. SHERMAN. And you are assuming they would not use nuclear weapons against their own people?

Mr. CHANG. Actually, they have threatened to do that because they threatened to nuke Taiwan which they believe is their 34th province. But apart from that, what we have seen China recently do is lash out. Not only against its neighbors, not only against the United States, but basically against everybody, and that does not make strategic sense. But it is an understandable tactic for leaders who are in trouble.

Mr. SHERMAN. It is the last refuge of every tyrant. If you can't deliver you can at least deliver impassioned nationalistic speeches.

You talked about a number of steps we could take on the trade front. Why wouldn't we designate them a currency manipulator except for the argument that they are manipulating their currency a little less now than they used to? Are they not still a currency manipulator and why have we not designated them as such?

Mr. CHANG. They still are, because almost every trading day the People's Bank of China is in the market influencing the Dollar/ Renminbi exchange rate. And under U.S. law we have a requirement to designate a country as a manipulator if it, in fact, manipulates its currency which China does, and it does so for a predatory trade purpose.

Wen Jiabao, who was Premier of China in 2008 or so, came to New York and basically said that they were manipulating their currency to keep their workers employed. And that is the definition of a predatory——

Mr. SHERMAN. I wish we cared as much about our workers. But go on.

Mr. CHANG. So we have an obligation under U.S. law to designate them a manipulator. That doesn't mean we have to do anything about it, but we should respect our own law. Because when the Chinese see that we don't respect our own law——

Mr. SHERMAN. You forgot the provisional law that says if Wall Street finds it inconvenient then it doesn't work.

Mr. Johnson, do you agree?

Mr. JOHNSON. I don't have anything to add to what Mr. Chang said.

Mr. SHERMAN. Okay. We have got a Foreign Corrupt Practices Act. It penalizes American companies that bribe Chinese officials. Presumably, this is for the benefit of the Chinese system. Does our enforcement of the Foreign Corrupt Practices Act with regard to U.S. companies doing business in China hurt us economically? Does it hurt or help us in other ways?

Mr. CHANG. I will let Mr. Johnson answer that question.

Mr. JOHNSON. No, I don't think it does hurt us economically. I mean this is how we project our values abroad. So I am a firm proponent of enforcement of the FCPA.

Mr. SHERMAN. Even with regard to protecting a regime from the corruption of corruption when we don't actually wish that regime well, at least many of us don't.

Mr. JOHNSON. Well, I don't think we would, even if that is true I don't think we would want our businesses engaging in corruption to help hasten its end if that is what you are suggesting.

Mr. SHERMAN. Undermine, I think, is a better phrase than hasten its end. Mr. Chang, do you have any different view?

Mr. CHANG. Long term, I absolutely agree with Mr. Johnson. Short term, you are right. On the short term, if we allowed U.S. companies to go bribe Chinese companies they would do very well. But long term that does hurt U.S. business not just in China but around the world. We learned that with the behavior of U.S. companies in Japan. I don't recommend it.

Mr. SHERMAN. I am looking for everything that might work. I yield back.

Mr. CHABOT. The gentleman's time has expired. I think this was a particularly good panel that we had here this afternoon, a good discussion, and thank you very much for enlightening us on a whole range of issues relative to our relationship with China. Members will have 5 days to supplement their statements or submit questions in writing. And if there is no further business to come before the committee, we are adjourned. Thank you very much.

[Whereupon, at 3:44 p.m., the subcommittee was adjourned.]

APPENDIX

MATERIAL SUBMITTED FOR THE RECORD

SUBCOMMITTEE HEARING NOTICE
COMMITTEE ON FOREIGN AFFAIRS
U.S. HOUSE OF REPRESENTATIVES
WASHINGTON, DC 20515-6128

Subcommittee on Asia and the Pacific
Steve Chabot (R-OH), Chairman

September 10, 2014

TO: MEMBERS OF THE COMMITTEE ON FOREIGN AFFAIRS

You are respectfully requested to attend an OPEN hearing of the Committee on Foreign Affairs, to be held by the Subcommittee on Asia and the Pacific in Room 2172 of the Rayburn House Office Building (and available live on the Committee website at www.foreignaffairs.house.gov):

DATE: Wednesday, September 17, 2014

TIME: 2:30 p.m.

SUBJECT: A New Era of U.S.-China Relations?

WITNESSES: Mr. Christopher K. Johnson
                   Senior Adviser and Freeman Chair in China Studies
                   Center for Strategic and International Studies

                   Mr. Gordon Chang
                   Author

By Direction of the Chairman

The Committee on Foreign Affairs seeks to make its facilities accessible to persons with disabilities. If you are in need of special accommodations, please call 202/225-5021 at least four business days in advance of the event, whenever practicable. Questions with regard to special accommodations in general (including availability of Committee materials in alternative formats and assistive listening devices) may be directed to the Committee.

COMMITTEE ON FOREIGN AFFAIRS

MINUTES OF SUBCOMMITTEE ON _____ *Asia & the Pacific* _____ HEARING

Day __*Wednesday*__ Date _____*9/17/2014*_____ Room _____*2172*_____

Starting Time __*2:20 p.m.*__ Ending Time __*3:45 p.m.*__

Recesses [____] (____to____) (____to____) (____to____) (____to____) (____to____) (____to____)

Presiding Member(s)

Chairman Steve Chabot (R-OH), Ranking Member Eni Faleomavaega (D-AS)

Check all of the following that apply:

Open Session ☑   Electronically Recorded (taped) ☑
Executive (closed) Session ☐   Stenographic Record ☑
Televised ☑

TITLE OF HEARING:

A New Era of U.S.-China Relations?

SUBCOMMITTEE MEMBERS PRESENT:

Rep. Ami Bera (D-CA), Rep. Brad Sherman (D-CA), Rep. Gerald Connolly (D-VA), Rep. Doug Collins (R-GA), Rep. Dana Rohrabacher (R-CA), Rep. Matt Salmon (R-AZ), Rep. Mo Brooks (R-AL),

---

NON-SUBCOMMITTEE MEMBERS PRESENT: *(Mark with an * if they are not members of full committee.)*

HEARING WITNESSES: Same as meeting notice attached? Yes ☑ No ☐
(If "no", please list below and include title, agency, department, or organization.)

STATEMENTS FOR THE RECORD: *(List any statements submitted for the record.)*

TIME SCHEDULED TO RECONVENE _____
or
TIME ADJOURNED __*3:45 p.m.*__

_____
Subcommittee Staff Director

Statement for the Record
Submitted by Mr. Connolly of Virginia

In the 21st century, U.S.-China bilateral relations have experienced increased economic integration and defense interactions. Despite increased ties on several fronts, the U.S. and China project two very different narratives in the Asia-Pacific. The U.S. strategy of engagement and its reliance upon international law and norms to establish a stabilizing presence in the Asia-Pacific is in direct competition, and at times, conflict with a Chinese strategy that is increasingly reliant upon coercion and unilateral actions and declarations. The future of U.S.-China relations will be defined by the extent to which the U.S. can sufficiently resource the strategic rebalance to the Asia-Pacific in order to expand U.S. influence while deescalating potential conflict.

U.S.-China relations are, without a doubt, on more sure footing that they were two decades ago. The economies of the United States and China are inextricably linked. In 1994, U.S.-China trade was valued at $48 billion. By 2013, it had increased to $562 billion to make China the United States' second largest trading partner. China was the largest supplier of goods imports to the U.S. in 2013, and the value of imported private commercial services rose 222% between 2002 and 2012 to $13 billon.

While security coordination with China remains limited by statute, there have been ways in which the U.S. has worked to cultivate a stable and transparent military-to-military relationship. U.S.-China security cooperation was completely suspended for 5 years following Tiananmen Square. This summer, China was a participant in RIMPAC 2014, a multinational maritime exercise that involved 22 nations and 25,000 personnel. China also joined for the first time this year the 33rd annual Cobra Gold military exercises in Thailand.

The limit to U.S.-China cooperation was illustrated in part by the mark up this Committee just concluded of the Ranking Member's legislation, H. Res. 714, concerning the peaceful and collaborative resolution of maritime and jurisdictional disputes in the South China Sea and the East China Sea. The legislation enumerated several provocative actions and declarations taken by China that undermine regional stability and disregard international norms. A notable instance of this troubling dynamic was China's establishment of an Air Defense Identification Zone (ADIZ) over the East China Sea in November 2013. The U.S. is seeking to establish regional stability in the Asia-Pacific by relying on an international order that is occasionally disregarded by a major regional actor. This is just one issue that the strategic rebalance must resolve.

Trade tensions are a persistent problem for U.S.-China relations. The U.S. has sought to relax these tensions with regional economic integration as well as dialogue with China. However, trade distortions such as weak intellectual protection rights, state-sponsored cyber espionage on U.S. corporations, and financial support of state-owned enterprises remain concerns. Establishing an economic order in the Asia-Pacific that rejects this bad behavior is one strategy for meeting this challenge. A tactic that supports that strategy would be the achievement of a high-standard Trans-Pacific Partnership (TPP) agreement. TPP would potentially affect almost 800 million consumers, approximately 40 percent of global GDP, and a third of global trade. TPP would allow the U.S., instead of China, to set the rules of trade for the region.

I thank the witnesses for their testimony this afternoon. I look forward to a robust discussion on the future of U.S.-China relations. With the right strategy and sufficient resources, we can achieve a more integrated and prosperous relationship with the Asia-Pacific while cultivating a stable relationship with China.